GO FACTS Physical science

Materials

A & C BLACK · LONDON

Materials

contents

© 2007 Blake Publishing
Additional Material © A & C Black Publishers Ltd 2008

First published in 2007 in Australia by Blake Education Pty Ltd.

This edition published 2008 in the United Kingdom by
A & C Black Publishers Ltd, 38 Soho Square, London W1D 3HB.

Hardback edition
ISBN 9781408102602

Paperback edition
ISBN 9781408104811

A CIP record for this book is available from the British Library.

Author: Ian Rohr
Publishers: Katy Pike
Editor: Mark Stafford
Design and layout by The Modern Art Production Group

Image credits: cover (main image) Shutterstock; p11 (bottom left)–NASA;
p15 (all)–Mark Stafford

Printed in China by WKT Company Ltd.

This book is produced using paper that is made from wood grown in
managed sustainable forests. It is natural, renewable and recyclable.
The logging and manufacturing processes conform to the environmental
regulations of the country of origin.

What are Materials?

Materials are what things are made of. Everything on Earth is made of materials.

Different materials have different **properties**. The properties of a material describe how it behaves. Does it burn or melt? Is it strong or weak? The way a material's **atoms** are arranged affects its properties.

Different properties are useful for different purposes. Metal **conducts** electricity, so it is used to make electrical wiring. Plastic doesn't conduct electricity, so it is used to cover wiring to protect people from electricity.

Some materials occur naturally in the ground, air, water and living things. These are called natural materials. Their properties can be changed to make them more useful. For example, wood can be dipped in chemicals to stop insects eating it.

Synthetic materials are made by combining natural materials. They are often made to act like natural materials, but with an extra property. Polyester is a synthetic fibre that looks like cotton, which is a natural fibre, but doesn't crease like cotton.

Property	Examples
floats in a liquid	wood
transfers heat and electricity	most metals
can be easily shaped, especially by rolling and hammering	gold, aluminium
returns to its original shape after being stretched	rubber, soft plastic
strong when being stretched	steel, silk

You can see the structure of materials with a magnifying glass or microscope. This is the surface of a piece of metal.

THE HARDEST
Diamond is the hardest natural material.

Wood is a natural material.

Wood

Wood is a natural material from living trees. It is made of plant cells.

Plant cells contain **cellulose**, a type of sugar. It links together to make wood fibres.

Wood burns easily. Its main use for thousands of years was as a fuel for cooking and heating. Wood is also used as a building material because it is strong and light compared to other building materials. One in four new houses in the UK are built using wooden frames.

Wood can be made into synthetic materials. Particle board or chipboard is made from pieces of wood mixed with wax and glue. Particle board is cheaper and denser than natural wood. It is used to line ceilings and walls and to make furniture.

Wood can be made into liquid paperboard, a special paper that can hold liquids.

Wood contains water. This spruce tree is about 80 per cent water.

Wood vibrates differently to other materials. It helps to give wooden instruments their special sound.

Paper is made from wood. It was first made in ancient Egypt from the papyrus plant.

Plastic

Plastic is a synthetic material made from oil.

There are hundreds of different types of plastic, divided into two main types – thermosets and thermoplastics.

Thermosets are very hard plastics, such as the ones used to make plastic chairs. They can only be shaped once.

Thermoplastics are soft plastics, such as the plastic film used to cover food. Thermoplastics can be heated, melted and reshaped many times. They are the most common plastics.

Some plastics resist heat and chemical damage. Others resist wear, so they are used in machines. Plastic can also be dyed many colours.

Plastic doesn't rot. Many plastics can be **recycled** or reused. Some new plastics are **biodegradable**. Those made from plant starch, not oil, will break down in soil. Plastic packing foam can be biodegradable – it will even dissolve in water.

Windsurfing boards can be made with plastic and fibreglass. Fibreglass is plastic with glass fibres added to make it stronger.

Plastic is used in artificial body parts, such as hip joints and blood vessels.

THE FIRST

Bakelite was the first widely used plastic. Invented in 1907, it was moulded into jewellery, radios, telephones and clocks.

In 1988, Australia was the first country to introduce plastic bank notes.

9

Glass

Glass is made by mixing sand, limestone and soda ash in a furnace. The **molten** glass is poured into a mould or laid out in sheets. It hardens as it cools.

Glass breaks easily. This property can be changed by adding chemicals or by changing the way glass cools. If you reheat glass, then quickly cool it, the glass becomes much stronger.

Pyrex glass is a special type of glass. It does not expand when it is heated as much as normal glass. The giant mirror in the Hale Telescope at Palomar Observatory in California, USA, is made of Pyrex glass. Pyrex was also used to make the windows of space capsules.

Glass is often used to hold food and drink. This is because the glass doesn't react with the things in the glass container and change their flavour.

Glass can be recycled over and over again.

Glass has a natural blue or green tint, which is caused by iron in the sand. It can be coloured by adding different metals.

Adding:	Colours the glass:
iron	green or amber
copper	turquoise
cobalt	blue
gold	red
uranium	yellow

Molten glass can be shaped by hand or by a machine.

A mirror is a sheet of glass with a thin layer of metal behind it. The mirrors in the Hubble Telescope have a layer of aluminium only 0.00008 millimetres thick.

Obsidian is a dark glass that occurs naturally. It is made when lava cools quickly.

GO FACT!
DID YOU KNOW?
Obsidian is used to make scalpel blades that are sharper than steel blades.

11

Metal

Most metals come from **minerals**. Rocks that contain minerals are called ores. They are crushed or heated to collect the metal.

Iron comes from iron ore. It is made into steel by adding **carbon**.

Most metals are shiny, dense and **malleable**.

Their atoms sit in an ordered pattern, like tiles on a wall. Metals are good conductors of electricity because **electrons** move freely past the atoms. They are also good conductors of heat.

Rust makes metal weaker.

Metals can **corrode**. When rust eats away at iron or steel, it corrodes. Rust is a flaky brown substance that forms when oxygen, water and iron combine. This process is faster if the water is salty.

An alloy is a mixture of metals. For example, stainless steel is an alloy of steel and chromium. Alloys have different properties – they can be stronger, lighter and softer than other metals. Stainless steel does not stain or rust as easily as ordinary steel.

Bronze is an alloy of copper and tin. It is often used to make sculptures.

Mercury, used in some thermo-meters, is the only metal that is a liquid at room temperature.

Ores are dug out of the ground.

MOST MALLEABLE

A single gram of gold can be beaten into a one square metre sheet.

13

A Good Conductor

Discover how metal conducts heat better than plastic.

You will need:

- warm water and chilled water
- two plastic spoons
- two metal spoons
- two cups made of the same material

Some metals conduct heat better than others. Copper is a very good conductor. It is often used to make cookware.

1 Fill one cup with warm water and one with chilled water.

2 Place a metal spoon and a plastic spoon in the warm water. Put the other two spoons in the chilled water. Leave the spoons in the cups for a few minutes.

3 Take out the spoons and feel their temperature on the back of your hand. One metal spoon will be warm and the other cold because metal is a good conductor of heat. The plastic spoons will be about the same temperature as they were before you put them in the cups.

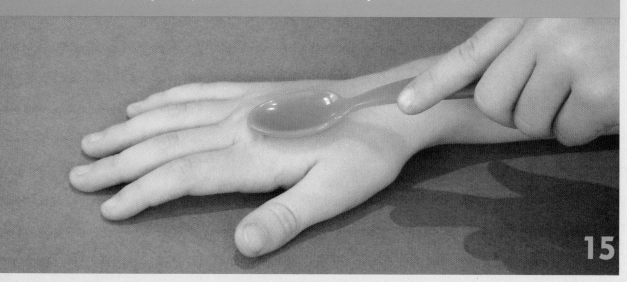

Fibres

Fibres are fine threads that can be made into cloth and ropes.

Natural fibres come from plants and animals. Linen is made from the flax plant. Cotton comes from the cotton plant. Wool is made from the **fleeces** of sheep and goats. Silk comes from the **cocoons** of silkworms.

Different natural fibres have different properties. Wool doesn't allow much air to move through its fibres, so it is warm to wear. Cotton lets air through, so it is cool to wear.

Synthetic fibres are made from oil. They are cheaper to make and stronger than natural fibres. Nylon and polyester are synthetic fibres.

Nylon was invented in 1935. It resists wear and damage from stains, moths and mildew. Nylon is a good material to make a raincoat from because it only absorbs 10 per cent of its weight in water. A raincoat made of cotton would absorb about 25 times its weight in water.

Natural and synthetic fibres are often woven together. This makes fabrics that have the best properties of both fibres.

One bale of cotton produces about 300 pairs of jeans.

Parachutes used to be made of silk because it is light and strong. Now, they are made of nylon.

Nylon is light but strong. It is used to make ropes and fishing nets.

Spandex is a synthetic fibre that stretches easily. It is used to make sports clothes and swimsuits.

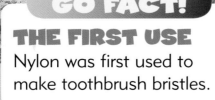

GO FACT!

THE FIRST USE

Nylon was first used to make toothbrush bristles.

17

Putting It All Together

Cars are made of many different materials.

The main metal in a car is steel. This gives the car strength. Metal alloys are used in engines because they are lighter than steel. They also handle the high temperatures inside an engine. Aluminium is sometimes used to make car frames because it is light and doesn't rust.

Plastic is used to make pipes and hoses and to cover electrical wiring. Plastic is lighter than metal, so the more plastic in a car, the lighter it is. Lighter cars use less fuel. This means they are less expensive to drive and produce less pollution. Cars in the future may have plastic panels instead of steel.

Interior:
plastic, metal

Lights:
glass, plastic

Wheel:
metal alloy

Tyres:
steel, rubber, nylon

18

The tyres on a Formula One car are made of nylon, polyester and very soft rubber. They last for only 200 kilometres (125 miles) of racing.

Soft roof: fabric, plastic

Windscreen wipers: metal, rubber

Mirror: glass, metal

Seatbelts: nylon

Seats: leather, plastic

Engine: aluminium, steel, plastic, rubber

Body: steel, plastic

19

Renewable materials can be re-made or regrown. Renewable materials include wood and natural fibres, such as wool.

Some materials are used much faster than they can be replaced. This means that one day they will run out. They are non-renewable.

Plastics are non-renewable because the oil they are made from took millions of years to form. One day we will run out of oil.

Some non-renewable materials, such as steel, plastics and glass, can be recycled. Recycling means that new materials don't have to be made.

Another way to conserve materials is to reuse them. Many things we use each day can be used over and over again.

The best way to conserve materials is to use less of them. Packaging is the main use of plastics. If people bought products with less packaging, we would conserve more oil.

Trees are often grown in plantations to be used for wood products.

It takes 40 to 350 million years for plants to turn into coal.

Reusable shopping bags and baskets can be used instead of supermarket plastic bags.

21

Building with Materials

Wood				
Glass				
Metal				
Plastic				

Glossary

atom	a very small piece of matter
biodegradable	will decay naturally by reacting with water and bacteria
carbon	a chemical substance in all plants and animals
cocoon	the soft cover that protects some insects as they grow
conduct	to allow electricity or heat to go through
corrode	to be eaten away by the action of air, water or a chemical
electron	an extremely small piece of matter with an electric charge
fleece	the coat from a sheep or similar animal
malleable	can be easily hammered or rolled
mineral	a chemical substance from the ground
molten	describes something that is in a liquid form because of heating
property	a feature of a material
recycled	when materials are treated to be used again
synthetic	describes materials that do not occur naturally

Index